All One Breath
Selected Poems

Harry C. Staley

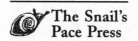

The Snail's
Pace Press

All One Breath

Selected Poems

For that which befalls the sons of men befalls beasts; even one thing befalls them: as one dies so dies the other; yea, they have all one breath.
                                        —Ecclesiastes

Harry C. Staley

The Snail's Pace Press, Inc.
85 Darwin Road
Cambridge, New York 12816
snail@poetic.com

Darby Penney, Publisher
Ken Denberg, Editor

The Snail's Pace Press is a member of the Council of Literary
Magazines and Presses (CLMP).

Front cover photograph: "Ancient Coral," Helen Raynes Staley
Back cover photograph: Helen Raynes Staley
Cover design: Darby Penney

**The Snail's
Pace Press**

ACKNOWLEDGEMENTS

Fourth Commandment *Psychopoetica*
Early Gothic, Obese as Buddha *Snail's Pace Review*
Brado, Caw *Groundswell*
The Rat (published as Requiescat), Penmanship *Berkshire Review*
The Final Flight *Arizona Quarterly*
Snorkeling , In the Nursing-Home *Open Mic*
About His Grandson, Cute Kelly's Semi-final, Puberty, Dennis
(Chips) Kelly on Pension, Spring 1938 (published as Gus Kelly
and the National Pastime) *Off Course*
About the Aeneid, Senile General *Albany Voices*
This Cold *Firebird*
That Year's Moon *Pennsylvania Literary Review*

I happily express my gratitude to the following, whose imagination
and intelligence inspired me over the years:

David Mitchell
Nate Leslie
Paul Grondahl
George Drew
George Szary
Michael Egan
Ken Denberg
Darby Penney
Ellen Reed
Dennis Collins
Patrick Burke
and Helen Raynes Staley, whom I'm still courting.

CONTENTS

CAIN & OTHER RELATIVES

UNCLE ORVILLE AND BEATRICE

From *The Lives of a Shell-Shocked Chaplain*

THOMAS KELLY

FOURTH COMMANDMENT

They started as giants huge and loving.

They diminished imperceptibly.
From the bedroom I heard the two of them
squabbling in the living-room.

I held on to beds and table-legs and chairs.
I learned to walk.

Hunting & gathering, my Father found
scudding on the pavement
a twenty-dollar bill.

8,000 Gum-Drops! 200 Loaves! 10 bottles of Gin!

A sporty God revealed himself
in the midst of depression.

I learned to pray.

In the time of hunger Hitler Hoover
God revealed himself.

By the time my father died
I was just his size.

        * * *   * * *   * * *

In sleep sometimes I try
to force them to apologize:

Father! you forgot to say thank you!
You left the table, the room, the world,
without excusing yourself!

Mother! Have you done your homework?
Never talk with your mouth full!
Keep covered; it's cold out.

Mom! Dad! Don't talk back to me!
Never ever talk back!
Never! Never! Ever!

All right! All right! You're grounded!
Just for that you're grounded!
How about THAT! Grounded forever!
Don't tell ME that's not fair!

Just wait till I'm your age Just you wait
You'll see...You'll see...

EARLY MISSION

I fly the Gotha past my bed,
soar above the reading lamp, and swoop
down toward the rocking-chair.

Looked upon from flight,
the shaggy rug tilts left, tilts right.
The surface of the floor lies flat
but violence seeths beneath
in the parlor just below.

The family's fighting there,
Central Powers, *Entente Cordial*,
fighting in the kitchen, in the parlor,
fighting everywhere,
Passchendaele, Armentieres, everywhere.

I dive down toward the table,
moderate reddish, well-scratched brown mahogany,
a target worth at least one bomb.
Down below the fighting rages on.
In the heat of battle someone shouts my name;
I drop the plane.

SNIPER

I draw a bead on Daddy's Nash.
K-CHOW!
I missed.
K-CHOW! Wounded him.
K-CHOW! K-CHOW!

DEAD!

Daddy, ignorant survivor, waves,
parks the car
and waves again.

BEYOND VICTORY

"What did you get [those medals] for?"
"For killing a lot of guys."
From *Beyond Victory*

I don't recall the movie, now,
but I recall the dream that night.
I watched myself, wounded and about to scream,
my family in another room, my Captain dead;
blood-stains spoiled my Christmas soldier-suit.

I saw me spewing luke-warm cream of wheat
on soggy lumps of mud in no-man's-land.
Face on the pillow, I heard me cry
for strong grown-ups to come and rescue me,
and scold the frightened soldiers on both sides.

Dawn rose upon a field of shining headstones,
spaced, rank and file, on gleaming blades of grass.
An eighty year old priest was celebrating mass.
My waking silenced him.

PUBERTY

FIRE TWO! I pulled the lanyard
one year after I couldn't learn the Lindy-Hop at
BLAM!
the Friday-Night-Confraternity-of-the-Christian-
Doctrine Dance
FIRE TWO!
Underneath the dresses and the lingerie,
the flesh bloomed lush and sacred,
full of grace.
BLAM!

Hundreds of fingers jerked the lanyards,
long hot muzzles blast off, blast-off,
blast-off, all over Europe.

Fire-mission, counter-battery done,
I shouted into space gone all but still,
"Was it good for you?"
thinking somewhere shameless blondes
lie prone and bleeding.

In a slit-trench dream
elegant skeletons danced in my skull,
flirting, despite their lost pudenda.
No flesh, no blood. Bone on bone,
they clicked and clattered all sleep long.

FIRST WILL AND TESTAMENT

[as required by Army regulations for those entering combat]

I, Corporal Kelly,
sound of mind, sound of body,
[*mens sana in corpore sana*]
one year after freshman-fall-semester, SJU,
[*vox clamantis in deserto*]
this Sixth of April, 1942,
bequeath:

To my Mother
a fistful of untolled rosary beads
and the notion that I still believe
[*Nate, quis indomitas tantus dolor excitat iras?*]

To my Father
the meaning of our muscles, flexed or limp.
Near-sighted now, he nods like Homer,
tries to remember the First World War
[*Dulce et decorum...etc*].

To the girl from whom I copied High-School Latin
and with whom I almost learned to love
[*puella? femina? Mulier?*]
I leave a cold and posthumous moon.

Note. Line 11: "Son, what great pain rouses thy indomitable rage?"
Aeneid, Bk II, 594.

TOM KELLY'S JOURNAL: TWO KILLS

[Jersey City, 1928]
Battles I fought in bed as a boy
roared me to sleep.
I, the perfect shot, slaughtered Turks and Germans,
almost every night, ignored wounds,
fought on until I fell.

       * * *   * * *   * * *

[Les Vosges, October '44]
Maternal, non-combatant, doomed,
the first dead I ever saw,
a cow-corpse on its side,
front leg fragile, taut,
pointing at us: *THEY* did it, *THEY*
did it.

Irrelevant fatality. I pictured steak
and milk and quiet pastures.

A man with nothing else to do
could snap the dead leg off,
and hear the bloodless crack.

We left her there still pointing,
"*Sieg Heil!*" Sgt. Gillyard said.
"a vegetarian like her *Feuhrer*"

       * * *   * * *   * * *

[Black Forest, April '45]
A perfect shot; above the eyes,
below the helmet and the hair.
Twelve years old. Slightly more?
Above the blood his hair was blond,
The uniform was not his size.
I turned away, stalking grown-ups

ENTREATY ['45]

Through the window I heard
twelve golden children lilt my pseudonym,
"Erich Von StROheim." My phoney name
offered them the afternoon before:

"Vie heisen zie?" "Erich Von Stroheim, *kinder*."
"Erich Von Stroheim?" *"Ja."*

"Erich Von StROheim... Eric Von StROheim..."
I, Erich Von Stroheim, AKA Cpl. Kelly, USA,
would I, a funny friendly guy, almost twenty-five,
wake up, get out of bed, come down and play?
Go down and play? I? Harold Ely, play?

I don't know. What would the grown-ups say?

NOSTALGIA BAR

for Mike Starrs

Nothing plaintive, nothing sad,
Nothing but the gay,
And lift the little glasses much
That we might greet the day
                    —an Old-Child's Song

Some nights:
we played with High-School Latin:
"Hic Haec Hokum..."
Caesar died with a swollen vocative:
Et TU?

Some nights:
I told tail-gunner tales, part fable and part farce:
"The target duly bombed, I counted stars
and raised my tenor voice
above the bomber's baritone,
all the way back to base."

Some nights
I sit and drink alone.

One night
there wasn't too much moon,
I started counting stars again,
golden, numberless, in the wide black cold.
Their heartless light, older far than Rome,
shone down upon the brief, surviving bunch of us.

VALOR

In childhood
and through most of puberty, I dreamed
I would be brave in the proud smoke of battle
and loved by healthy girls whose flesh I'd spare
by wounding other flesh

and I believed
whatever weapon pierced my flesh,
bullet, shrapnel, sword, or bayonet, renewed
the sacred penetrations that sanctify the world:

Adam in Paradise
Cain at the plow
Mary and her Ghost
the nails that pinioned Christ

But once in war I came to know
I was outranked by any child
great moonlight bombers slew

PROFESSOR KELLY

...the mind arises as a result of physical interactions...ranging from the molecular to the social.

— Gerald M. Edelman

INVOCATION

Sing, heavenly Moose! Make thou the depth
of swollen midnight darkness risible.
I pine for paronomastic brilliancies
provoking laughter preternatural,
monstrous undulations of giggle and guffaw
as though old Aeolus and some companion gods
of flatulence and storm send gasps
and gusts of wind that, gathering, explode
in ruthless hurricane across the lawns
of Troy, and Rome, and Gloversville, New York.
O Horned God of Comedy, I beg
the balm of wide approval and applause.

A LETTER FROM TOM KELLY, SR.

My breath fogs a bit of windowpane
as I look out, half-hoping you'll be there,
walking up the lane,
staring at the house, staring at the door.

You always stared ahead to where you meant to get:
out of the crib, out of the bed,
out to the weatherside of the windowpane.

Now you stare through new vicinities
in their exciting climate, I suppose;
strange and novel landscapes
provocative and beckoning
beyond the reach of my old love,
my weathered voice.

I shout against the wall sometimes
toward where I think you may have gone.

I see a sphere
bright on the trunk where the heavy branch had been.
Time has healed it to a kind of crust;
I think it was the wind that wiped it smooth and clean.
But the branch is gone.

Huddling here in base-board heat
I feel the cold;
despite the thermostat
I feel the cold,

A private winter's working
in my bones, and in my blood.

I stare against the weather of my memory,
feeling cold.

SNORKELING

> ...but the fear exists,
> *Delenda est Carthago* on the rose horizon
> —Derek Walcott

I, too, scan the bottom, tracing old
embattled landscapes, and, yes, among them
Cato's Africa, revived in high-school Latin,
and among them even old Manhattan,
long before it found its "iron ground."

But I'd rather watch the fish.
From time to time they play like schoolmates
flashing as they try to learn
the wordless syntax of their shallows.
Through every surge of current, every turn
of tide, their "time" is simply now.

Or so I've come to think, as I,
an aging Yankee in a young and wealthy country,
repeat the pompous "passive periphrastic,"
Delenda est Carthago. Well, I suppose
history threatens each *Carthago,*
call it Rome, Jerusalem, Baghdad, or Chicago,

even as I float above the fish, a chubby God,
soft and horizontal, belly slightly scarred,
watching plunge and pivot, dance and dart.

THE RAT

Walking down the cemetery road
I came upon the body of a rat
spared by scavengers, apparently intact
in open air beside the buried dead.

Prosperous paunch,
a silent bulge against the tarmac black,
its blacker tail
tapered toward the roadside trench.

I hate rats. Shrewd, they scrounge through filth
and prosper, giggling, squealing, nibbling,
in ghetto walls, or barns, or scuttling
through fetid fields of death.

Not this one, for a moment, not this one
still soft to sight. I saw its corpse
like someone slain you trip across,
enemy or friend, after battle's done,

field-rations clumped in the dead crop,
stiffening away like any mortal man,
like any guy, every lust, every hope,
every instinct, gone.

KELLY AND SOME GRAVES

> *St. Moling built a little church called*
> *"Templenaboe." In former times*
> *unbaptized children were buried there.*

In St. Moling's grave-yard   Kelly spied
three small globes,
each with a crucifix inside:

A dead white Y   on a bright black cross,
luke-warm liquid   shining glass.

He stole the globe   on the farthest left,
Patron Ghost   of the damned and lost,
who'd bad-mouthed Christ   and paid the cost.

He brought the Thief   to Templenaboe
placed the globe   above children's bones
under weeds,   dead branches,   wordless stones,
who wait for the   Apocalypse
and nowhere to go.

OBESE AS BUDDHA

> *Poets, remember your skeleton. In youth*
> *or dotage remain as light as ashes.*
> —Kay Boyle

Obese as Buddha, I betray my bones,
slim and burdened under bulge and bulge of flesh,
a living, obscene burial.

Poet with tenure, I snorkel on sabbatical,
a plump and pompous blimp over swift
and slender fish; never far from shore and sandwiches.

A social square, a bloated sphere,
a pudding paradox, I would appear
narrow and rectangular.

Despite the glee of gluttony, I want to be
proud as Freud, zensitive as Kerouac,
with the sleek libido of a shark.

INTERROGATING THE Ph.D.-PROPOSAL

Demythdefying, defable-izing
every yarn of barn or bastion
choralled in the old abandoned pastures:
there won't be, were not, are not
few sure pastorals in our presence
every monetary be swarms away
and the flies of textures are upon U
wend a re-dun-dance of engine histree
scents all the tragic eros
rolling prone and supineless tunhill
to hades and gentle-sex off one and dozing off tether
obfuscating on thin I's
with the high source writerless and none
to read a read a meter made
but the mighty misty-flying epic Theorist
putses best footnote forward in hirs post-ductural feces
the purplish or pear-ish apple source, the vestigial appendix
afall human history
from the snack in desanctifying grass
Till the study of the study of the study of
the last lost problemicised and blasted
inturdeggschewall canonicity.

PUNTHEISM

> I gag on jargon, but it pays my way;
> it is deeply creative to exploit a cliché
> —Dr. Sigmund Jung

Lacan is up to his old catoptrics;
furthermore, his is a false image in his own Lacan-glass.
My ex-therapist is non-directive and Lacanic.
She told me I am not the only one to pun on nuns,
but to dream nun-puns is idiopathic.
Almost every night nuns tell me to eschew gum.
I tell them I never eschew anything I can swallow.
They tell me to stop punning about them.
I assure them I'll kick the habit.
They remind me that pious ejaculations,
that is to say, intense little prayers,
help prevent sins of emission.
And whenever I feel like sinning
I should ask the Blessed Virgin to help me.

My counselor informed me that Lacan makes all this clear.
"The diagnosis is simple:
You are muddle-aged;
Your nunnage is complicating your dotage;
therefore,
since you have a debt-wish, keep a budget
and respect the treasure principle.
You want to deride Derrida. DON'T!
Take comfort in Lacan's maxim:
'We see ourselves in a glass starkly.'
After a few more sessions you won't need to pun;
you won't have nun problems at all.
Remember,
puns are the lowest farm of humus;
Punsters are dishonest, totally freudulent!"

LACANAGAIN

Mendacious as mirrors, as memory.
image on a red-brick wall
image in the wind
the piss in epistemology.
the sip in insipid.
lacan with the wind

ABOUT LOWER CASE

he sent his talk-poem toward the capitals of the earth
  preaching the cult of lower case
and except for inverted commas all his punctuation
  was
        space

once or twice he seemed to think it nice
to *italicize* and i guess i find it
negatively grand that he never used the ampersand
well in one talk-poem at least

i kinda guess that i m the kinda guy
who likes to leave every bit of lint unpicked
and every hair unsplit ask my barber ask my tailor
but i note that someone adorned a talk-poem title
with a coupla caps like this

"Radical Coherency"

and after the final lyrical lower-case verse
there hangs a little asterisk

i suppose or maybe i kinda guess nobody *speaks* in up—
or low—er case but i cant tell by listening
whether commas are more like time than space

but i believe in immanent, not transcendent, meditation
not *t*-m but *i*-m
and only a liberal- dilletante- anarchist would let them
place an asterisk
after a talk-poem and cap the title

but i think hes gonna collect all unused
capitals and commas and semicolons and apostrophes and periods
and save the earth and a lotta other things because

hes a regular kinda poet slightly outta kerouack
an unpedantic sorta writer who thinks of himself
as a kinda reader who makes each talk-poem
as vatic as jerry meyer long ago

TOM KELLY MIMICS R-B-RTS-N D-V--S

See here—I might qualify
as an artist, poet, gleeman,
mightn't I?
Something of your intellectual?
Well, possibly? Well?

And *I*
find not the slightest difficulty
in Christianity
its beauty, and its mystery.

Mary's conception was and is immaculate?
Why not?
Dry and clean and true
as your Hemingway might say?
Why not?

Macula non est in te
Catholic children sing those words
Macula non est in te
Listen to them. Listen.
Macula non est in te
For Heaven's sake,
Why not? See here,
Why not? Eh?

MUSEUM

The figures have no significance as individuals,
only elements in form and colour. The red and
white of the woman accentuate the depth of the
archway... long since vanished.
   —Hermine Van Guldener, *Rijksmuseum*
   Amsterdam Paintings

...long-since vanished:
that woman, red-and-white. Mrs Siess, perhaps,
who lived, I think, across the street;
long since vanished, no significance at all.

My memory's gone all sepia.
I recall her days in blurs of dull nostalgia
set in late December, early March,
"only elements of form and colour
dissolving in the hazy atmosphere."

I remember something more of Mrs Siess:
her daughter said she lost her place
in a chapter that approached despair
before the happy-ending in God's grace.
Almost there, she lost her place.

Her daughter said her heart-beat simply stopped.
At the age of fifty-eight
in the middle of a night
and the middle of a book she never finished
her heart-beat simply stopped.
Something invisible had vanished:
"Self," her daughter said; "or Soul,"
had abandoned what lay thoughtless on the bed.

I think I can compose the room:
The book lay open on her chest;
by her bed the reading lamp still shone
upon her Savior, gazing from the wall,
his Burning Heart a fist-sized candle in his breast.

Neither gaze nor candle fluttered as she died.
With dawn the lamp-light barely reached the wall
and Christ, his Heart still burning,
stared across the room
where nothing moved except the clock.

CONSTRUING *ALIQUIS*

I don't care about her, never did.
In Latin 4 we were assigned to give
an English version of her flaming suicide
as she cursed Aeneas, false and fugitive.

I got an A for that. To celebrate
I ordered shish-ka-bob and chomped it down
with a glass or two of coke. But
of all the words I struggled with, just one

worked long enough, worked north and west enough
to vex me even now. I can't construe the word,
can't match it with the fury of her love
(Brother Victor didn't "do" the word).

Helpless, broken-hearted, there it lies:
Someone, Something, Anyone, arise.

NEVER SAY DIDO

I look for rum in Rome,
a warm cafe for those like me
who know a song or two.

Taberna est in oppidum, oppidum.
There! Hear that!
There is a tavern in the town.
I ask to join. "You pass,"
they say. "You pass."
I carouse with Latin Regents!
I! Ego! I!

She enters the cafe:
every breath of old-space changed.
Her scornful eyes are aimed
at every one, at anyone, at me.
I translate into schoolboy prose
the torment of this jilted Queen,
ruthless and unsatisfied.

Let there be no love
let them fight, and their children fight
and the children of their children's children

My words drone on the page, boring and grammatical;
but the Regents say I pass.

REST ENERGY AND THE DOE

> *All matter possesses enormous "rest-energy"*
> — Nigel Calder, *Einstein's Universe*

From somewhere in the upper woods
a single burst
pierced the dark around my house
and woke some nervous dogs
and me.

Next day my summer world held calm enough,
clear, composed, and nearly motionless;
but (if I believed a book I didn't understand)
charged with its own dumb energy.
Angry implications in ordinary space.

In *that* stillness, *I* held still,
gazing from the porch through quiet light,
down along the sloping lawn
to the shaded company of trees
a stride or two beyond
the shiny surface of the pond.

The doe intruded gently from the copse
at the bottom of the lawn;
there followed one, and then another, fawn
thirsty, hungry, irresponsible.
Now and then I seemed to sense her scold
as she watched them splash and sip and nibble.
Loving them, she listened to the silence
in the potent world surrounding them,
ready for whatever might be lurking there,
like me.

They passed quite near the porch.
She stopped and briefly contemplated me.
I thought I saw resentment in her eyes
before she turned away and led them off
toward the upper woods where everything,
just then, seemed still.

ABOUT HIS GRANDSON

He runs ahead of me. I call him back.
"Stay near me, Steve, until we reach the park."
He no longer toddles, loves to run
until he's out of breath. "Stay near me, Steve,
it's almost, almost dark."

I'd like to tell him "Paradise" means "walled-in park"
where no one ever had to feel ashamed
and none were ever old enough to totter,
and beauty was not yet sin-deep,
and none would sense a pun in "out-of-breath."
Long before the apple and the snake,
long before the scepter and the orb.

He runs ahead of me toward years and days
and afternoons I'll never know. Even so
I try to call him back. Even so,
call him back and stay forever
in the daylight in the park.

PNEUMATICS

Pneuma: *breath, spirit, soul,*
that which is blown or breathed.

Something flows away.
Not like the luke-warm breath
in old balloons we played with once.
Small quick bursts that made me cry.
And quite unlike the hiss of air
when they fluttered, crazy, through the room,
striking wall and bed and chair,
sagging down at last
limp and flaccid on the floor.

I think of death sometimes when I think
of flight. Sometimes...
Once near summer's end I watched a bird
clearly dancing to her own delight,
a solo turn beyond all words, all jargon,
no "thermal currents," only shining summer air,
sheer joy, high glee, and wild control.

Whatever broke her dance I can't explain.
Her music changed, perhaps, or stopped.
I heard no shot,
but what took place was quick,
a drop of breathless weight,
an empty lump that briefly shocked
the flowing branches of a willow tree.

CONVALESCENT

I left the ward "barely fixed,"
Scotch-tape safety-pins a little glue,
staples and a tack or two,
my bones so many twigs and sticks.

The maples had shed for winter,
December skeletons, freezing on the lawn
in cold clean space.

As late as August, juicy green,
they'd sparkled through the pane,
before the symptoms, red and brown,
glowed on dying leaves.

So, at least, lying in the bedroom,

I remembered them, as I seemed to feel
soul and mind and memory,
all one transparence, easing toward
a fine and final otherness,
all-encomposing, voluptuous.

I heard words they'd made me memorize
years and years before: "All one breath."
The beasts and I, and the birds that fled the cold
while leaves were letting go:
"All one breath."

A SERMON KELLY NEVER HEARD

Cecidit de coelo stella parva
—distorted from *Revelation*

A small star falls, still shining.

Now Listen!
In the beginning will be the Word
Genesis succeeds Apocalypse;
God anticipates what happens long ago,
as Ecclesiastes says.

The small star shines forever, falls again, shines on;
the breath of God still moves upon the waters.

Meantime you Faithful dip your hand
in luke-warm water,
to bless yourselves.

Do it as you think of death
and clock-time ticking
toward contradictions of eternity

when once again you'll wait
in the starless space before your birth.

WAITING FOR BECKETT

He was having us on. What he was doing
was having us
on.
Had us on
and now he's gone
like THAT.

Space shrank toward him. That's what happened.
Space
narrowed to nothing.
The old horizon closed inside
the unsurrounding center of the world.
Center swallowed circumference.
That's what happened;
scape lost scope:

World-scape, sky-scape, sea-scape,
land-scape, room scape, skull-scape,
ZERO.

There's no *here* here
now that he's gone there.
There?   Gone there? Where?
We don't know where. Anywhere.
So there!

Nothing itself happens there.
There is where nothing is itself.

vale atque ave

Something here, then? Listen...

Something? Here?

Having us on?

Listen...

COMA

for Tom Kelly, Prof. Emeritus

I touched your brow and wondered...
a conscious nothing darkening?
A another pun for me that never quite escaped?
Unlikely fragments out of Tao:
"deep...it's darkly visible...it only seems..."?

       ***   ***   ***

I'll flee the final stitch of time
and fly through vehement winds
past the geese of the kingdom
beyond the farthest rim of space

Bright stars stare inside my dream until
dawn works grey in the haze of my head
gleaning through synaptic guesspells:

Matthew-Mark-Luke-and-Warm:
this is the scene where I came in,
when all is sad in dawn.
I'll shovel off this mortal soil.

II

Was there a kind of etymon in matter
and we, so many names, its progeny?
An utterance before sound,
no word yet possible,
and SHE was there, the Etymom?

Precursor molecules spawned us;
progeny through energy in rock,
ancestors, pre-syllabic, pre-subjective,
dumb but fecund? Atom then Eve?

...Eve and, lighter than air,
the human mind
(attitude and craft):

slabs and lintels,
Stonehenge,
Attic ruins in forgotten sunlight
(bright broken beauty, shining still)

the few teeth left in a pauper's mouth,
dentures in my Father's water-glass,
sleek shapes of steel, soaring, sensing,
shattering,

and the mushy tangled brain inside my skull,
about to dry away and suffocate
the memory of Molly Kule,
the Mother of us all.

WAKING TOWARDS THE LAST DECEMBER

Nomads Land! Sguarll and squeeks in the fearist.
Cant see the floress for the freeze:
      The daze of the mumps mismumbled
      as the sleaves on the breeze autumbled.
      They are misflamed, miscountered.

O, let the Viatic come.
Pop Prelatzers and whine to fry
in the lowest fright of angels.
Oh for one auGUST of wind! One ice septender tray!
The last placemeal! The lost treadmeal!
Oh, munch the whole-wheat white-attic crumb!

Drowned in deep-ocean, drained of devotion,
a weed to the wide is surf-fishing:
"In the Beckoning was the Void."

Those were his lost birds,
flown through the winter-pain of death
He dried sceneless. All his mortal sense forsaken.
      Oh, the underscraper will scour his skin
      till the scars shine.
      His day that rose in dusk unto dusk it is interrned.

ELEGY FOR THOMAS KELLY

Ah, Tom, what are metaphors but fertile lies?
You'd say "This" is "That," and hope
the loving world believed. It tries.

Precocious still in later middle-age,
a timeless *wunderkind*, you memorized
each day. Each day you learned your part,
reliving even as you lived.
Invoking old Euhemerus,
you got down every day by heart,
embellished for retelling.

Tom, we're both still boasting in the yard
after school lets out,
Miltonic metaphors meant to readjust
the ways of God to us;
metaphors, not similes.
Valiant lies
we even bring to bed with us
to fill the time it takes to fall asleep
proud, naive, and credulous.

Well Tom,
every "That" has come at last to "This":
We're working to preserve contending versions of your memory.
We're reaching, Tom, for every one of you.
Come home and tell us all you did or might have done,
or all we know you did not do.
Tell us now, before the night gives way
to one more ordinary day.

CAIN AND OTHER RELATIVES

CAIN

Remember, Abel murdered first, killed a "creature,"
one our Father Adam named
after we were made to leave
the walled-in park where Eve,
our Mother,
shared with him the fruit of knowledge
and made us mortal.
He named us all: Tiger, Turtle, Serpent,
Lamb
named me "Creature," Abel "Son,"
every creature named, every single one;
but none was slain until
Abel offered God his kill
and God approved.

I never fattened calf or lamb for sacrifice.
I, named "Creature," knew each beast
even as I knew myself.
I offered bread and wine,
crust and juice, nothing in disguise,
no hidden clots or scars.
My apples stored no guilt.

Among His avatars, I venerated Ceres, hated Mars.
I consecrated bloodless feasts
to celebrate the harvest, sang "Te Deum Laudamus"
and left each lamb of God feeding in the field.

I SLEW ABEL

and it came to pass that the Lord destroyed every
living substance, "both man, and cattle,
and the creeping things,
and the fowl of the heavens,
and they were destroyed from the earth
and Noah only remained alive."

I slew Abel
And it came to pass that Abraham meant to slay Isaac
and the Lord said, "because thou hast not withheld thy son,
thine only son,
I will bless thee."

I slew Abel
And it came to pass that the Psalmist sang,
"Happy shall he be that taketh and dasheth
the little ones against the stones."

TWO MEALS

And it came to pass:
        Chips Kelly waked to the rage of whirling birds
        screeching near his window;
        saw the sparrow-hawk stun a fledgling rook
        rise & strike again,
        hold the vague-eyed creature down, clutched in claw,
        bite through feathers, bite through skin,
        wrench off gobs of flesh,

    skirr off, slaked and buoyant.
    skinny skeleton and skull
    useless in the fading rage.

        Chips scrambled eggs for breakfast.

CUTE KELLY'S SEMI-FINAL

Chips hears a housefly thud against the pane
a bit above a spider web,
buzz back and turn and hit again
and lumber off in shock,
perplexed by hard transparencies,
sophisticated space.

Chips remembers Cute, his brother, jabbed and jabbing,
red gloves smashing swollen flesh,
blood across his eye;

lost six straight and quit for good
mumbled into waves of buzzing space,
a puzzled yearning in his gaze.

The fly writhes, fighting in the web;
Chips squashes it against the sill,
more to spare the little jerk than kill.

DENNIS (CHIPS) KELLY ON PENSION

Sleeping in his rocker, Chips walks his beat,
glazed streets in gaslight
littered with thugs and thieves;
bastards, murderous bastards, battered and prone.
Chips blows the whistle, clubs the curb,
waits for the Lads to come
and cart the garbage off. He waits alone.

The rocker creaks;
lips pursed, he stirs, fist clenched and empty.
Whatever that was, it was not the Lads.
Eyeing a sinister window,
he blows the whistle, clubs the curb again.

Down the street a rag-time slut
hears the noise and strolls away.
He waits alone.

Where are the Lads?
The rocker creaks
and wakes him to the room,
quiet, blurred, and warm.
He sees the glossy windowpane
this side of everybody else's night.
Where are the Lads?
Nobody heeds him anymore.

Patchy Pete, the one-eyed cat,
prowls the alley, snarling and secure.

UNCLE GUS KELLY

1. Spring 1938

Toward the very last, almost dead,
Gus Kelly,
[Baseball-fan, Salesman, Poker-man, *St. John's Alumnus*] said,

"The cards God dealt were low,
mostly spades, none really wild,
and none of them, none of them, a joker.

"I had" he said, "a paradox for openers, and a rare
deck of baseball cards for sentimental solitaire
when nobody else, nobody else, nobody else was there.
Not Zeke Bonura, not Bordagoray, not
"Boots' Poffengerger, not 'Blubber' Malone.
I was alone.

"Not Hal Schumacher, 17,
Not Mel Ott, (number 3? Number 8?)
I watched *those* two play a nearly perfect game.
They were great. They were great
(cheap bleacher-seat for maybe half-a-buck
in Ebbets Field in '38. In 1938.).

"'Schumie' shut them out; And Mel Ott shot
a big one into Bedford for the only score.
And Rosen, Goody Rosen, got...Rosen got?
...the only Dodger hit.

"He was erased at second base.
I don't recall his number; I don't recall his face,
but he was erased, all right,
at second base, a double-play,
'twin-killing' they sometimes say. .
Oh, he was erased!

"I ran across their names again
in Zinnser's history course:
Eugen Ott, who served the Reich,
a general, a diplomat.
And a Schumacher named Kurt,
who lost a leg
from torture in a concentration camp.
A Socialist, Zinnser sneered. A Social Democrat.

"For all I know,
there might have been a Jew named Rosen, squeezed
inside a box-car with a number on his arm;
more digits than on Goody's uniform.

"On the day I watched the game
I'd never heard of them.
I was a fan; I watched the game.

"As for history: I suppose
The Brooklyn Eagle's 'Morgue' has Goody's name
somewhere in a box-score.

"Nowadays they mostly play at night;
but the lights are going out
and I forget the score,
or maybe I don't care.
And nobody else is there; just me alone.
Nobody else is there.
And maybe I don't care."

2. Nuncs

Time is a succession of nuncs
—Aquinas, perhaps.

I'm running out of nuncs. Running out.
They were beautiful, a few of them;

Some guys had a basket-full, some a box,
some a little paper bag,
and one of them a handful in his pocket;
I forget his name.
Father Brood said he'd save them for his coffin
and for the after-life
where there's a lot of them,
a Jacob's pot of them.

What do they look like? Nuncs?
They're transparent. Brief. They're infinitesmal...
They leave on arrival.

UNCLE ORVILE AND BEATRICE

LITURGY: Father, Fowl, and Daughter

> *In general, flying signifies transformation*
> *from a worse state to a better, and hence*
> *renewal and rebirth.*
>
> —C.G.Jung

Orville Ely,
assiduous and apron-clad, bastes with seasoned sauce
a tender chicken, slain and smouldering on the coals.
He favors recipes from Zosimus
or any ancient alchemist
whose cooking methods Jung preserved for us:

> *Take a fowl [volatile]*
> *cut off its head with a fiery sword*
> *pluck out its feathers, then separate*
> *its limbs and cook it slow*
> *over a charcoal fire till the bird*
> *burns down at last to a single shade.*

His guests and family gather on the lawn,
eager to swallow the sacrifice
and praise the host, partly to atone
with him who sweats a bit
over blood and body, spice and sauce,
brooding till the crackling sizzles down.

Atone? At one
in the afternoon?
With whom? With him? With Ely?

> *...a fair-haired man with dark-blue eyes*
> *immersed in a jar of sesame oil*
> *was fed with figs for forty days...*
> *they tore off his head and packed it round*
> *with cotton wool and placed it on*
> *burnt olive-ash. Its eyes could see*
> *but the lids could not move,*
> *it revealed to the people their inmost thought.*

Sipping from his glass at last,
he sees his daughter Beatrice munch a wing
and watch a turkey-vulture hunger through the air.

   ...in order to renew the moon-goddess
   a maiden was decapitated, skinned;
   a youth then put the skin around him
   to represent the goddess, risen once again.

Bird and girl adorn the afternoon.
As Orville stares the vulture out of sight,
some words of Bryant touch his "inmost thought":
... *abyss of heaven... swallowed up thy form.*
He shifts his stare to Beatrice and her grin;
this time she wants a leg, without the skin.

---

note: Quotations from C.G.Jung "Transformation Symbols in the Mass," *Papers from the Eranos Yearbooks* Vol. II.

PRINCIPAL PARTS: ORVILLE ELY

Day in day out, night after night,
School-Superintendent Ely searched for Bea, little Bea,
even for the Bea that ran away, sulked off,
bad grammar, new nubility, cheap,
sulked off, in a rage of raucous music
after the last retarded tantrum,

from a home where
he could bathe himself clean as his grammar
where the soap smelled moral
the porcelain looked Protestant;
linen and shirt and soul, all unstained,
he worshipped a clean-cut Christ.

Grace was said before each meal
one mistake in grammar earned an insult
two mistakes in grammar earned a slap,
three mistakes in grammar sent one from the table.
Grace was offered after every meal.

...Searched for months through scummy neighborhoods and streets
reeking like latrines
Orville Ely,
well-dressed and terrified,
assaulted by the sight of life-sized dolls,
pneumatic, in flimsy, dirty lingerie,
plump and sickening, as large as Bea,
in shops that smelled of sweat and sin and urine.

Home again beside his well-washed wife
his dream sinks inside Manhattan Harbor;
pollution stains the porcelain teeth,
the swelling eyes, the gills, the membranes,
the delicate entrails of edible fish;

pollution taints the alleyways and avenues,
contaminates the breath and lungs and brains
of pigeons, pimps, and prostitutes, and the heart of prowling Ely.
His right arm long and mean,
blemished with tattoos, he prowls,
young again, silky mean, the long arm
and the mean hand like a poison-snake,
angry fingers clutching the mean knife;
Ely aches for victims, for pimps, fags,
pigeons, johns, pneumatic dolls,
runaways, runaways, runaways,
to go, going, went, GONE,
all one victim, androgynous as zeppelins,
one infected soul sloughing off in sobs of fog,
Ely himself the wounding I,
the wounded me.

ABOUT BEATRICE

1. Beatrice Remembers Her Mother

Sometimes, singing me to sleep, she sang too well
and made me cry.

She sang beyond the ceiling and the moon,
she sang me past the harmony of stars,
through old expansions of the world,
through depths of midnight, and the breadth of days.
She sang into my future where I heard,
and hear, ambiguous refrains.

She sang past mountain-clouds and castle-clouds
past blues of summer near the lake,
toward winter and the silence of our life
in empty rooms abandoned long ago
where even now she's singing me to sleep
knowing where I've gone and where I go.

2. Beatrice Trip

he tranced off into my tomorrow
leaving me here in his yesterday
I'm gonna find me a friend and borrow
money for shit and blast away
earn me a sinister A K A

Christ is rocking on the mantelpiece
struttin' his stuff in a seamless gown
rehearsing an act with a coupla thieves
gonna rock & roll all over town

the bad thief drums and the good plays fiddle
with a single & a double & a triple paradiddle
sideman satan's gonna bring me down
sideman satan's gonna bring me down

3. Beatrice: Feast of the Epiphany 1948

Asleep in the street near a People's Drugstore
dreaming of milk in a shiny white bowl
I pissed in the pants I had pissed in before
while two angry angels fought for my soul

God took on flesh (so they say) in the winter
swaddled immortal and not very old
sucking soft breasts and warm in the manger
he pissed like a human asleep in the cold

4. Beatrice: *Essence* & Accident

As a child she believed
the silent hum of god
in empty black solitude
spawned a breadth of space
exploding into history

Later priests and shrinks
tried to squeak their minds
to her
      (to *her*
waking to a different trauma,
invoking puns
even as they squoke)

No one heard the car brake squeal
and screech beyond her gasp
her last silent scream of consciousness

Hum is where the heart was

5. Beatrice in Surgery

The old diminished hum,
there, down there, underneath the coma,
underneath the clip, dip, snip, snap,
there, inside the shining blood, inside
the secret hollows of memory and bone
sinking past a final resonance
sounding out toward spaceless black
surrounding history.

Frightened, I shiver back to flesh,
and vulgar harmony, the mortal synthesis
of sight and sound
                    I hear a voice
implore a mourner to rejoice:
"... he'll shine before the glory of the Beatif..."

Pain wrenches through my waking guts and moves me to forgive.

6. Hic Jacet Beatrice

Beatrice gone,
Orville Ely comments to his son:

"This is the way she remembered us.
Well no, she never told *me* how she remembered us.
But the friend of the therapist to whom she told it
    explained to my colleague who recounted to me that
'This is the way she remembered us.'

"I think my colleague (sensing through the words of the friend
    how deeply impressed the therapist was with the way she
    remembered us), was touched.
Which is to say, my colleague and his friend and the therapist,
    were not indifferent to my daughter's memory.
I find some solace thinking about these three.

"I have no image of the face of the therapist, or his friend.
My colleague, as he talked to me, seemed to stare at his
    impression of my face.

"The therapist saw my daughter's face, although
    my colleague and his friend did not.
They were given a careful version of her words
of which I have their paraphrase.

"I try to fit the face they say the therapist said he saw
with the drifting faces I recall:
One face says 'I can shay anyshing!'
One face cries at halloween.
One face only stares.

"I try to fit the faces with the paraphrase
...one face only stares."

from *The Lives of a Shell-Shocked Chaplain*

PENMANSHIP (1931, 1984)

OOOOOOOOOOOOOOOOOOOOOOOOOOOOOOO
IIIIIIIIIIIIIIIIIIIIIIIIIIIIIIIIIIIIIIIIIIIIIIIIIIIIIIIIIIIIII

He (I) dipped the pen-nib into the blue ink-well,
inscribing all we'd need to know
in lovely cursive servile script.

He (I) trained in Palmer-Method
ovals and pushpulls
by the Sisters of the Iron Cross

aware of sin slithering near
beautifully tattooed
(ovals and pushpulls).

Nuns and pupils (we) drove the serpent off
with quick ejaculations, and God (numinous, austere)
forgave.

Already longing backward from my future, he (I)
wooed my approbation, mine and all the tall appraisers,
nuns and priests and God (ubiquitous), everywhere,

everywhere, their evaluating stare:

in sleep,
with Vera, Mary, Grace and Gloria, tracing ovals;
he (I) making pushpulls

in dreams,
he (I) hide in oval shell-holes;
then, brave in no-man's-land, he (I) push

metal bayonets into German guts, and pull
the wet blade free
before we wake and wash
and walk to school.

SERVICES (1929)

I.

After Black Thursday the light began to change.
October grew dim in offices and stores
and the nervous eyes of relatives.

Sunday Charles attended Children's Mass,
lulled by Latin; carefully Young Father Smith
revealed the host,
omnipotent and bright,
larger than a quarter.

In the vestibule Old Father Smith
who would outlive his troubled sight
waited for the end of Mass
to watch the children pass him by,
his one eye blind, the other sad.

II. Vietnam, 1966

Even as I hold aloft the unscarred disk
I understand the holy rage of Cain
who laid the harvest of his heart,
the yield of earth and seed,
bloodless wine and bloodless grain,
before the sanguinary eye of God

who found such sacrifice unworthy of his name
and vouchsafed his regard
on Abel's immolated Lamb,
a slaughtered creature, its shy heart stilled
to satisfy the hungers of the Lord.

The transubstantiated host holds Christ de-stigmatized:
the wounds are gone,
the wine won't scab, the bread won't scar,
there's nothing there for Thomas' hand to touch
unlike the bodies of the faithful, kneeling here
and swallowing; whose warm and mortal blood
absorbs the sacrament, and courses on a little longer.

BIOLOGY ONE (1934, 1957)

Brother Gilbert intoned: "Boys, Ah boys!
Remember Ruth, and forget about old Darwin."

who was, we knew, an atheist and kinda foreign
and claimed we came from apes
who came from fish who learned to fly
or crawl and climb old trees and then climb down again
and learned to walk upright and use the thumb
and think and talk and master Latin
and pitch and HIT HOME RUNS, "Ah, the Babe, boys!"

Just last night, still hearing him, I sank through sleep
and illiterate leagues of ancient oceans, down
to the salty womb of everyone. There
a killer whale, deeply aloft, aware of spotlights
shining in high night,
stares through tides and surging centuries,
metamorphoses and nests, spires and temporary towers,
soaring chambers of power deeply aloft in high night
above the last vast evaporation and the blank
obituaries of

tigers orioles cardinals cubs
giants indians senators reds
braves pirates
Boston, Brooklyn, Washington, New York:
THE YANKEES, "Ah, the Babe!"

ASYMPTOTE (1945)

(A line which continually approaches a given curve, but
does not meet it within a finite distance.)

You must remember this as time goes by:

as time goes by there'll come a time
when time will start to STOP going by
and when it stops the bogeys go
but that won't matter,
you won't know.

* * *   * * *   * * *

In April 1944
Cpl. Cyril Marowitz tore
the limbs and head from a musical doll
(dressed in a German uniform)

He spared its trunk so we all could hear
the pain of its delicate tune.
Marowitz died of artillery vibes
on a noisy afternoon,
nobody noticed the doll was gone.

* * *   * * *   * * *

It's still the same old story:

You can't know the locus of a point, kid,
where the crazy curve of life, kid,
hits the crazy line of death.

* * *   * * *   * * *

Bogey   an imaginary source of fear
Bogey   a bugbear
Bogey   an evil goblin
Bogey   a screen image that is unidentified, but hostile

IMMERSION

He still dreams he's learning how to swim
while grown-ups on the beach
encourage him.

These days he dreams alone; no one on the shore,
breathing ordinary air,
needs or cares to care.

He yearns to yearn once more
towards something he has yet to learn,
something brave that he has never done,
rehearsed in dreams and then
performed at last by day.

He tends to sleep through shallow waters now
far from the deepest volumes where
deep-sea scrawls
hold tales of tide-lost gallantries
read by children,

not by him. He sounds the depths in vain
and, nothing fathomed, surfaces to dawn.

DARK CUBES

But of the cities of these people,
which the Lord thy God doth give thee
for an inheritance, thou shalt
save alive nothing that breatheth:
But thou shalt utterly destroy them
                              —Deut. 20:16

In one dark cube or another, in the movies, in the bedroom,
my old dreams batter humanity,
an almost anonymous slaughter with a few elegant names,
Ayres, Baxter, Bosworth, Clive...

Dr. Oscar Homolka, the psychoanalist,
warned of rage in heaven and homicidal paranoia,
but nobody guessed his sweating hysteria
possessed a Balkan truth even as silver Zeppelins
eased, smooth, through cold space,
nudging darkness, piercing night,
toward Paris, London, toward our diocese,
into dreams between the walls, between the wars,
Spaniards slaughter Spaniards in fiction, film, and barrio,
while *THE HINDENBURG* sails east.
And later, somewhere else (between the walls),
paratroops descend like doomsday angels
killing sinners, sparing saints:
choirs of maggots cleanse the battlefield
leaving bits of boneshine
unlike splattered shreds of flesh and muddy corpses
left to dry in Belleau Woods,
                         and nothing like the living frog
I killed in Summer 1932, a lump
of soggy camouflage, her astounded eyes the size
of BB's that, *phump-phump,* did the job
in the lovely light of early afternoon.

MORNING SONG

...then *pit* inside my sleep, slight,
isolated, *pit*, then another outside,
sharp, isolated, like battle opening beyond the windowpane,
light rain, hesitant, uncertain,
drops deepen like open vowels,
farther back and lower in the throat,
pit, bled, blood,
they concentrate, rattling under
high rounds of thunder
blasting overhead
like battles fought from soft seats
in the movies of my childhood,
artillery mixed with musketry
killing scores of valiant youth
in blazing black-and-white

     in nineteen forty-four "somewhere in France,"
     Norton Ipswich Alexander,
     whom we privates and corporals called
     Ipswich
     because we liked the sound of it,

          died

     his real, three-dimensional jaw torn away, the blood
     spread red, searching cold space
     for something warm to heal
     flesh, or cartilage, or bone, somewhere in France,

     his death, I remember,
     was the very first of very few
     in a quiet sector

movie wounds are frightful, but
I don't know what Norton felt, fading quick, unlike
the film star, draped on barbed wire all night long,
while other actors pray for him to die

dignified generals praise their dead; sometimes
I try to picture them with shattered jaws, like Norton,
or this morning's mouse, taut and cooling in the trap

That might be what woke me just before the storm,
something in another room
went like *that*

ABOUT THE AENEID

Exoriare aliquis nostris ex ossibus ultor
(Arise some avenger from our bones.)

Although my mastery of Latin fades,
that Queen translates herself forever
into fire, an angry light
for cold imperilled voyagers;
that classic blaze dims down
to prosody and syntax
fluttering in dactyls.

And I, a later voyager, over fifty years adrift,
contemplate the grammar, not the pain,
of burning bones and vengeance;
I who claim to be incensed
about the burning bones in MyLai,
after Belsen, Nagasaki, Watts,
and Washington.

What then of Dido's pyre? She
and the language of her love are dead
while modern fires seethe
where proud and pious syllables
(El Salvador, Granada, Concepcion, Colon)
mark the reach of recent empire.

Aliquis...ultor? Some avenger?

From the holy ash of "pagan" bones, napalmed far away,
let some surviving love
redeem the years of sacrilege
while we God-fearing Christians study all night long
to parse the meaning of our bombs.

EARLY GOTHIC

Remember adolescence?
mired in masturbation, secret years
of solipsistic orgies. Think:
His eye is on the spasm.

Sr. Thomasine rebuked our tearless eyes as she,
wallowing in pain and piety, her angry lenses
flashing grief,

described
the grisly bloody tortured death of Christ one thunderous
Friday afternoon years and years and years ago
and RIGHT NOW this rainy wednesday morning
GOD
once colorless odorless tasteless lighter than air
hangs NOW
only thirty years or so
after Christmas and the cold night of Epiphany
after scores of paupers and poppas played Santa

GOD
made up as Christ, bruised and torn and stretched
(ambiguously moribund),

and we murder Him with sin
gazing at Grace Black, Mary Fleisch, Vera Potter, Gloria Gales
(in their precocious loveliness),
We, prolong and share the very act of sacrilege,
of deicide and desire
done by Adam, done by Eve,
who brought original filth into the stainless world
we, Adam-and-Eve; we, Grace, Mary, Vera, Gloria; and we
who gaze at them,
longing.

TIDINGS (Christmas 1930's, 1973)

Having missed the early plane to Endicott,
I heard the engines hum and roar
and watched what looked like oil-slicks in my cup.
I missed the safe geography I'd learned in school
and hymns my classmates sang in unison.

I missed the cheap electric train that turned
and turned and turned

(from ENDicott to WAVerly & BINGhamton
      & ITHaca
& BINGhamton & WAVerly & HOME again
to ENDicott beneath the Christmas Tree),

transporting nervous relatives in shabby overcoats
and sweaty hats, who drank from cardboard coffee-cups.
The kind of men who
missed

sleek model planes that roamed out loud
through epic corridors at home, when I,
the GOGGLED ACE, held bombers in my hand,
my humming heard in Flanders Fields and Hollywood,
humming over table-tops and chairs,
over Dresden, London, Nagasaki, Troy,
humming after trains near Endicott.

CAW

I try to hold my sleep against the dawn

I sleep against the outside light where crows
(nuns and Sergeants   priests and colonels)
conspire in the brightening yard
calling me from play calling me from flight
back through the pillow calling me from flight
beyond Saigon, beyond Hanoi, and Seoul
calling me from flight
I fly high beyond the call
cursing God for every shattered wall

I sleep against the clarifying day   against a plebiscite
of murdered selves forgotten relatives and mean
authorities bleeding friends parents and parishioners
conspiring with a squad of crows
to call me back again to call me down
to call me back to call and call and call

VOLTAGES AND A FADING COAL

> *...a spiritual state very like to*
> *that cardiac condition which the Italian*
> *physiologist Luige Galvani, using a*
> *phrase almost as beautiful as Shelley's,*
> *called the enchantment of the heart*
>   —Stephen Dedalus

Once in June
lightning rang my telephone

Once in childhood
I touched a socket with my fingertips
and felt omnipotence
buzzing through my bone

Late in the Enlightenment
damp muscles in Galvani's frog
twitched and shuddered to the charge
of a "weak metallic arc"

In the eighteen-hundreds Emerson spoke of *dream-power*
transcending all limit and privacy
by virtue of which
a man is a conductor of
the whole river of electricity

In the Summer of 1953 the radio announced
Ethel and Julius Rosenberg had been
electrocuted

post-mortem examinations of electrocuted criminals
revealed
a number of interesting phenomena
the temperature of the body rose promptly after death

the heart
at first flaccid when exposed
gradually contracted and assumed a tetanized condition

the blood was profoundly altered biochemically
it was of a very dark color
            and rarely coagulated

Sometimes at night
something in my head goes PING
a brainspark blows my dream;
I wake to smokeless dark
unscorched
and turn to find my love

FISH, TWO GROWN-UPS, CHRIST (1975)

I shave this semblance of my Father's face
and staunch some blood my razor caught

I see him on his knees one brilliant summer afternoon
building us a dock with nails and wood
where later on I caught and scraped and gutted fish.

That sacrifice of living time and flesh,
the nails and wood, and now my bit of blood,
revive the rage of Sister Thomasine,
rigorous nun, whose reading of the death of Christ
set her eyes aflame with blame.

Father and nun. Digested by the earth long since,
they sift through particles
of sand, perhaps, or wood, or the knees of penitents,
or even through the drifting heft of fish
like those I imaged in the hearth last night,
orange perch, shadowy bass, minnows smoldering,
and near the bottom, wall-eyes glittering.

Sister Thomasine,
I no longer cry for Christ;
I see my father in my aging face,
I staunch our blood.

PARAKEET AND PILOT (1979)

Nearly dead, she will not sing her flight, this trifle
in the corner of the room,
losing the little heat that all the living lose.

Unlike my childhood dream of flight
decades ago: the helpless *ALBATROS*, gaudy fuselage aflame,
propellor feathering,
burning back to earth in Europe's smoke
while I salute and roar away.

Now, a cold bird gone,
I clean the cage.

HALLOWE'EN

It's late enough, my private ghosts and guisers have withdrawn,
they beg no more, play no more pranks;
the past has stopped arriving,
even in my dreams. A spectral absence haunts
me now, near dawn.

Saints succeed in their indifferent way.
They've nothing to resolve in these old haunts;
they've left the neighborhood
for good.
      What creaks and shimmers through the walls
is hardly holy, hardly sinister,
a beam, perhaps, or stair, or banister,
innocent, aging, crepitant.

Meantime the pumpkin grins upon the windowsill,
seedless, plump, and like the rest of us
(save ghosts and saints, or souls
burning in purge or doom), like the rest of us,
bio-degradable.
      Above his toothless grin, eyes
glitter, giddy, through the glass.

        * * *   * * *   * * *

Just before I slept, I thought I heard,
oh, somewhere past the edge of town,
a red stag roar in late October rut.

LATE WINTERS

1. This Cold

This cold, he knew, was only seasonal.
All things held still and centering,
wood tightened in the trees and wall,
earth hardened in the hollow and the hill:
mere wintering.

In that moment of the mute and beautiful
he heard across the cold a shallow call,
that held the heat and need of some lone animal,
drift soft and wandering.

2. That Year's Moon

That year's moon went wild with autumn, caught
some men alone and made them mad.
He was alone, but he was winter-wise
and kept indoors to nourish what he had
of warmer memory against the last surprise
that had to come to make his memory naught.

He had a hearth and bed and one large chair,
and all his friends lacked shadows, sat austere,
awaiting amends he'd set his mind to make
as priest, as friend, and from a recent fear
that they were more than shadowless. The lake
began to thaw, snow smoked; he held them there.

Then winter was, like him, another thing
old. And with the warmth he let them go,
unsatisfied with his apologies.
The empty chair, dark hearth, and vernal flow
sent him to bed without his memories.
The icicles cracked and died with spring.

IN THE NURSING-HOME

1. The Senile General In the Garden

hears the names of flowers bursting out
from war-games in his childhood "near the Somme"
peTUNia! beGONia! peTUNia! peTUNia!

from field maneuvers staged in Tennessee
peTUNia! beGONia! rose-rose-rose! peTUNia! peTUNia!

from battles in the 40's near the Rhine
rose-rose-rose beGONia! BLOOM! rose-rose.

BLOOM! peTUNia!
BLOOM! BLOOM-BLOOM!

a few far-off poppies,
and in the silence, a vision of the proud
gladiolus.

2. The Senile General Contemplates a Snail

your cave lurked dim beyond my dew
air billow cases soared us loft
glazed were the creeps our mergings knew
in the gracious daze we donned and oft

O morning stain that marked our stealth!
O wistfulness! O west cargo!
weren't we one dear innershell
on pulsing bed one live chateau?

a taintair and belivered sigh
I offer all who laugh then lapse
and you with your cold and stoning eye
I kiss in my apocalypse

3. McCaffery's Solitaire (Nurse's notes)

from 1 P.M. to 2:15 he played
a kind of solitaire with six or so
uncertain photographs
he thumbed them down with care

complained about a missing
ACE
was told to wait

complained he could not see their
EYES
was told to look again

played a round of "faces wild"
complained about a missing
SPADE
was told to wait

complained about a missing
CHUCK
was told the chuck was there

exclaimed he was about to
CHEAT
was told to go ahead

complained about a missing
CHILD
was told the child was there

at 2:15 began to whimper
asked for different cards

THE FINAL FLIGHT

The final flight was quite uncertain.
I accounted for the shift of shadow
because the window curtain
that kept dusk solemn in the meadow
shivered from the sill;
I saw the meadow. It was still.

I had been certain that with human death
there is, invisibly, the final flight,
swift with the anguish of the latest breath
and birds shriek wildly in the night.
I was one to watch him die.
These legends lie.

The little flame above the candle glittered
evenly. I thought it best to leave.
There reached us muffled through the curtain
the common song a late bird uttered
wild with life and very brief.
The final flight is quite uncertain.

Colophon

All One Breath: Selected Poems was set in a computer version of Caslon. The original Caslon typeface was cut by the English typefounder William Caslon and was first shown in his specimen of 1734; it was re-cut by the Monotype Corporation in 1915. This book was printed by A&M Printers in Cambridge, New York.

Other Poetry Titles from the Snail's Pace Press

Field Guide to the Ineffable: Poems on Marcel Duchamp
by Grace Bauer.
These highly original, intelligent poems based on the life and work of
French surrealist Marcel Duchamp are witty and surprising. The
poems evoke not only the spirit of Duchamp, but the best of con-
temporary American poetry.
32 pages, perfect-bound   (sold out)

Green Tombs to Jupiter by Barry Ballard
Barry Ballard's collection of lyrical blank verse sonnets inhabit
contemporary settings and tell stories with precise imagery and
metaphor. His poems have appeared in *American Literary
Review, Midwestern Quarterly, Paris/Atlantic,* and *Barbaric Yawp.*
32 pages, perfect-bound   (sold out)

Fishbone by Aimee Nezhukumatathil
From pickpockets to peacocks, elephant rides to electrocuted oysters,
Aimee Nezukamatathil's debut collection teases the uncommon out
of the commonplace, the miraculous out of the mundane. These
poems are luscious and sharp, full of severe irony and eloquence.
32 pages, perfect-bound $7.95/$9.00 post-paid

Four Nails by Gaylord Brewer
Gaylord Brewer writes with wit, humanity, and a sense of what
matters in life. Like good whisky, these poems go down smooth,
then kick.
88 pages, perfect-bound, $12.95/$15.00 post-paid

Snail's Pace Press
85 Darwin Road
Cambridge, New York   12816
snail@poetic.com

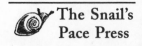

The Snail's
Pace Press